Everything You Need to Know About:

E COLLAR TRAINING

By Larry Krohn

MAINTENANCE PHASE

This is when the dog is off leash reliable
E collar is there (if needed)
Can bounce back to intermittent phase to practice

INTERMITTENT PHASE

4 Combinations:
1. E Collar with reward   3. No E Collar with reward
2. E Collar no reward   4. No E Collar no reward

Practice Everywhere:

Start adding distance duration and distractions
In this phase dog learns to respond with and without E Collar
(Stay in this phase if necessary)

CONDITIONING PHASE

Use the E Collar with every command
Reward every time
Train with as little distractions as possible
Keep sessions 5 to 15 minutes
3 to 7 days on average
Recall and place during this phase

TABLE OF CONTENTS

What you are about to read is everything you ever wanted to know about training dogs with the use of an e collar or remote collar. We will use the term e collar throughout. The e collar is the greatest tool ever created for dog training with the exception of the leash. Yes the leash. Without the leash, great e collar work would be more difficult. Unfortunately, the e collar is also the most misused, abused, and misunderstood tool in the world of dog training. It is basically what the Pit Bull Terrier is to the dog world. It is the tool mostly attacked by the purely positive community and has been banned in some countries as of today. If you are a bad dog trainer, an e collar will make you worse. If you are a good dog trainer, an e collar will make you better. It is that simple, but please keep in mind it is only a tool. One tool in your arsenal of tools, methods, and techniques that is useless without an overall good training program.

As we move forward we will discuss everything related to the e collar. We will go over step by step instructions on how to condition the dog properly to the e collar. Basically, how we teach the dog to understand this very foreign stimulus that can be quite confusing to the dog. We will go over what we do once the dog is conditioned and understands the language of the e collar. We will discuss how we implement the tool to an overall training program. We will talk about how the e collar can be used to reinforce known behaviors as well as how it is used to stop unwanted behaviors. Also, we will go over the most popular questions I receive on a daily basis and I will provide answers to them all. I will also provide a list of many useful training tips that will aid in your training and use of the e collar. At the end of our time together my goal is that anyone that reads this will have all the information and knowledge they need to greatly improve your skills with the e collar and as a dog trainer.

Almost 40 years ago I was introduced to my first e collar. I was a young kid and an avid pheasant hunter. I saw bird dogs out in the field not responding to their owner's calls. I witnessed a lot of yelling and screaming followed by a push of a button on the e collar remote while their dogs would be yelping and screaming and running back with their heads down and cowering. I hated it and I swore I would never use that type of collar on my dogs.

Fast forward many years later. I saw my first video on the internet of a dog trainer training his dog using an e collar. The dog did not look like it was being harmed. In fact the dog looked great. I became obsessed and started watching every video I could find and researching anything related to e collars. There was not much out there especially compared to today, but I found everything ever written or documented and became even more curious.

My wife pushed me to go meet one of the trainers I was watching with all my free time. I was still skeptical and was hesitant to put an e collar on my own dog. I would never do anything to cause any harm or mistrust with my dogs. NEVER.

I met with the trainer and we talked. He asked if I wanted him to work my dog. I thought about it for a second and decided to give it a shot. My dog took to it very well. Instant focus and he looked sharp. I knew instantly I would be adding a new tool to my tool box.

From that day on the e collar was used on every dog I trained except for puppies under 6 months old. I had tremendous success with the tool and my popularity as a trainer was rising. I started getting calls from a lot of other trainers that wanted to learn from me. I worked with many and usually free of charge. It was important to me that they learned the proper use so they would not be harming dogs. I knew a few of them already were doing some pretty bad e collar work and I felt like I had to change that.

Back then I thought the training was perfect. It was not. It was good but not perfect. At that time, we were still using too much pressure and not yet combining the e collar with food reward as we do today. Sometimes the dogs could look down in the dumps for a couple of days. Unfortunately, there are still many trainers that use the tool this outdated way. Also, what people have to understand is a lot of trainers learned how to use the e collar from watching YouTube videos. That is literally the extent of their training. Most never ask what their background is and pay a lot of money for a level of service they could have done their self.

Over the years, I have been fortunate enough to have traveled and worked with many of the best in the business. I learned from all of them and still do. I have been extremely outspoken about improper use of the tool and have taken a lot of heat for it. It is important to me that we keep the right to use our tools, all tools, but if some don't change their ways there is a very good chance we will lose them just as they have in other places.

Today e collar training is combined with positive reinforcement to create beautiful harmony. Whether it is the use of a clicker or a verbal marker, combining the use of both is pure magic.

Let's get started on the conditioning process.

CONDITIONING THE DOG TO THE E COLLAR

Here I will discuss how I start the training. It is very important to teach the dog the meaning or language of the e collar. The stimulation is completely foreign to the dog and if you want the highest results possible you must teach the dog the language. I will cover how I handle board and trains vs private lessons. Let's get started.

Let's assume the dog knows nothing. We are starting from the beginning. I want to teach the dog a marker word. It can be any word. I use YES as I know many others do also. You can also use a clicker but many find it difficult to work a clicker, remote, and reward with food all at the same time.

I will stand in front of the dog. A hungry dog works best. I will say YES, with an emphasis on the marker word and then give a food reward immediately AFTER the marker word. It is important to reward after and not at the same time as the marker. I will do this maybe 10 to 20 times. Just to give the dog an idea that something good happens when it hears YES.

At this time, I have the dog on a 10-foot line attached to usually a flat buckle collar. I used a 15-foot line for many years but I find that too many people have trouble handling that long of a line without getting it tangled up under the dog. A ten-foot line gets you enough distance for the dog to move about and is easier to handle.

Using straight line pressure when the dog is away from me I say COME and with very gentle straight line guidance assist the dog toward me. You want to use the lightest pressure possible and when the dog starts to turn toward you give the marker word YES and reward with high value food when the dog gets to you. By straight line pressure I mean that the leash is parallel to the ground or lower from where it is attached to the dog. You want to mark the initial behavior of the dog turning to come to you. With the dog knowing the marker word this should make the dog move to you with excitement. If the dog decides to veer off or stop just continue to guide with the leash.

If I am training a board and train I will take the first day just hanging out and building the relationship with the dog. I will also use light leash pressure to communicate where I want the dog. I will also work a lot of doorways, or thresholds. I want to teach the dog to just be. Be in a good state of mind and hang with me. Put your trust in me and don't worry about anything.

If I am starting a private session client I will start the straight-line pressure with the COME command and reward immediately after the ten or 20 repetitions of the marker word paired with the food reward. Also since time is limited, I start the e collar conditioning about half way through the ninety minute first session.

Now it is time to put the e collar on the dog and start the teaching process.

First I brush the dog's neck very well with a Furminator removing all dead hair. Dead hair will prevent good contact. Next I place the e collar on the dog's neck. You can place it anywhere on the neck below the ears except on the larynx of the dog which is under the neck right in the middle. Place it off to one side or the other. I actually prefer it placed very high just under the ear on most dogs, especially dogs with thick coats or thick skin. It just seems easier to make good contact up high. Make sure your leash is attached to a regular collar, not the e collar. Never put the leash on the e collar. You don't want to pull on the e collar.

One of the biggest mistakes people make is keeping the e collar too loose. You have to have it very snug or you will not make good contact and even worse inconsistent contact. You should barely be able to get two fingers under the e collar strap, not the receiver.

Now that the e collar is on the dog you are ready to find the dog's working level. This is best to do in an area where there is little or no distractions if possible and on pavement instead of grass. Too many odors on grass and if there are distractions your dog's working level will be higher than he actually feels it without any distractions present. Remember we want to use the lowest level possible that the dog can feel. Barely feel is what we want.

Start on the lowest setting of your e collar. You should have a high quality name brand e collar. Don't skimp here because a low budget e collar can create many problems such as inconsistent stimulation and the lowest levels can be too high for your dog to train properly and HUMANELY.

With your dog not paying attention tap the e collar. I keep my e collars set on continuous but still just use it as a tap meaning it is only continuous if you hold the button down which we are not here. Continue raising the level and tapping the collar until you see a sign that your dog feels it. That sign can be very subtle so pay close attention. It may be just a flick of the ear, a lick of the lips, or a dog may stop breathing with his mouth open. It can be more obvious, like the dog may look behind him trying to figure out what that weird feeling is. All of these signs are normal. Once he gives you a sign that is where you want to start the conditioning. Once you start and the dog has been feeling it, you may even be able to go down a little lower in levels once the dog becomes sensitive to the feeling.

Now we are ready. I condition the dog two ways as many of you know. Here we will use the continuous just as a tap after the command and we will also use the continuous held down before the command. Many ask why both ways. It is simple. Because it works. It works very well. Years ago I started doing it both ways after working with a very well-known dog trainer. He was doing it this way and when I see the best in the world doing something I pay attention. Everything I do has come from people far superior to me. The trainers you never see promoting themselves because they don't have to. Actually when I started conditioning it this way it was an instant game changer. Incredible results even faster than I was already achieving and the dogs looked great.

Just like we did with the leash work and come command we will now do the same but with the e collar in use. It does not matter which you do first, but in the beginning, we will separate the two ways the e collar is used meaning after the command or before. Let's start before first.

With the dog not paying attention to you, press and hold the continuous button down, give the come command and if necessary assist with very light straight line guidance. As soon as the dog turns to move toward you, release the button on the e collar and mark with a big YES. Reward when the dog gets to you. If the dog stops half way to you or veers off, it is ok. Just reapply the button and assist the dog to you. Our goal is to make it easy and help the dog as much as needed to succeed. Remember to mark as soon as the dog turns, not when he gets to you. Knowing the marker word should build speed in the dog since he knows something good is coming. Continue practicing this way for 5 to 10 minutes. Keep it very short. End the session with a nice walk or play but no e collar use. At this point the e collar will only be utilized when training. The dog will have it on as long as you are with him. If he is to have it on for several hours make sure to move it to another part of the neck so the dog does not get irritated where the collar sits on the neck. Also the dog will not have the e collar on at night to sleep.

This should go without saying but make sure you have a treat pouch on and high value treats. You have to be set up to work smoothly and with minimal effort. I use Red Barn and Natural Balance Food Rolls. Dogs love both and both are very convenient.

Now after the dog has rested for at least 30 minutes we are ready for another session. This time we will use the e collar, set on continuous still, but as a tap after the command.

With the dog not paying attention, give the COME command, tap the e collar right after the command even if the dog is coming to you while providing light leash guidance if necessary. As soon as the dog turns mark with a big YES and reward when he gets to you. If the dog does not come immediately or veers off just use a tap tap tap in a smooth and not machine gun rushed cadence until the dog complies. Again 5 or 10 minutes and then put the dog up to rest until the next session.

For the first day or two keep the sessions separated meaning only using the collar before or after the command. After a couple of days you can integrate both ways. Once the dog is trained completely I never use the e collar before the command. At that point, the maintenance phase it is only used after the command when the dog does not comply. Also for the first couple of days I am only using the recall to teach the meaning of the e collar. Lots of repetitions, over and over. As the dog begins to understand the stimulation I will add the place command also. I will teach the place command first through positive reinforcement. I like to teach opposite movements meaning teach the dog to come to you but also teach the dog to move away from you. Very important in training and too many trainers don't do that. I teach nothing with the e collar. EVERYTHING is taught through motivation, food mostly, but toys and praise if needed.

A couple of other things I like to do during the early stages of conditioning are: Stand in front of the dog, with no commands, no talking and with the e collar on the working level just tap the e collar and reward with food. Repeat several times. Click and treat except instead of a clicker you are using the remote collar. The other thing I call turnabouts. While walking at a good pace down the street with a loose leash, dog can be next to you or a little ahead of you, do a complete 180 degree turn and tap the e collar at the same time. Again, no commands no talking. Just turn and tap. This is sending your dog a signal to just follow you when the light stimulation is felt without a command telling the dog otherwise. For the turnabout, I am not marking or rewarding. Just silence and nonverbal communication. This is a very effective technique.

There will be dogs that have zero food motivation. That is ok, we do what we must do. Usually they will be motivated by food once they are comfortable with you and the training. If not then we just use praise. It is ok. Don't stress.

You should plan on training in the conditioning phase for a few days. Once you see the dog doing well and responding consistently we can move to what I think is the most important phase, the intermittent phase. This can be anywhere from 3 days to a week. It depends on your ability and the ability for the dog to learn from you. There is no right or wrong time frame here as long as you give the conditioning phase a few days at least. Also, don't forget to use the e collar every time in this phase and reward every time also for the recall and place command if it was taught.

INTERMITTENT PHASE

This is the phase where we really start pushing the dog a little more in the training. During the intermittent phase, we will start to add distance, distractions, and duration. This is also where we start preparing the dog to respond to commands whether the e collar is on or not. That is where many people fail. I hear it every day. They say my dog responds with the e collar on but when it is not he blows me off. Very common and most likely not enough time was spent in the intermittent phase or actually none at all. You can now also start using the e collar on all the basic commands that your dog knows well, such as come, sit, down, and place. In this phase, you will not be using the e collar every time you give a command and you will not be rewarding with food every time you give a command. We will work through four combinations of reward and e collar use. The four combinations are as follows:

E collar with reward: Example, Give command with use of the e collar and give food reward when performed

E collar without reward: Example, give command with use of e collar but this time don't give a reward. The dog must hold the command until released.

No e collar with reward: Example, give a command without using the e collar and reward with food when performed

No e collar no reward: Example, give a command without use of the e collar and without rewarding with food. Dog most hold command until released.

Practice these four combinations in any order. You do not have to use any specific pattern here, just mix it up. You will be in this phase for as long as you need to be. Don't be in a hurry to move to the last phase which is the maintenance phase. The maintenance phase is where the dog will have the collar on and you will use it only if you need to. Practice in the intermittent phase as much as possible. Start adding duration to the commands the dog knows. Start adding distance to the commands the dog knows and most important start training in different places around real distractions. Add distance, duration and distractions a little at a time. Don't go from giving your dog a place command from next to an object to trying to send him to a place from 30 feet away. Start from 1 foot away, then two, then five feet away. Think baby steps and a little at a time. It is a marathon not a sprint. Same with duration and distractions. A little at a time builds up very quick. Keep working in the four combinations during this phase. This is where you also want to spread out the food rewards further apart. The dog should never know when the reward is going to come. It should be a big happy surprise when it happens. Keep training fun and productive.

During the intermittent phase I also like to practice with the e collar on long walks. This is one of the best things you can do. You will have plenty of opportunities to test your ability and test where the dog is at in his training. During these walks, I use a good structured walk at times, where the dog must be at my side with a loose leash and just following me. During a structured walk there is no peeing, pooping, or sniffing until I find a spot where I want the dog to go. At that time, I will give the release command and the dog can go enjoy himself however he wishes.

When not in a structured walk I will use a 20 foot or more leash so the dog can move about freely if he stays close enough for my liking which is no further than the length of the leash. During the free walk, I will practice the dog's recall, especially when distractions are present. This is something that must be done before you let your dog off leash. If your dog blows you off while on leash he is not ready to be off leash.

Keep in mind that during these walks it is important to have the collar set on the appropriate level. If your dog works on a level six on a Mini Educator around your home without distractions then you don't want to go for your walk with the remote set on a six. You may want it on a 15 or 20, or even a 30. The number is not important, the response is. You keep the e collar set on the number that your dog will respond to around real distractions. You don't want to wait until your dog blows you off to start searching for the right level. BE PREPARED FOR WHAT IF.

Here is an example of what may happen when you first start your walks with real distractions. Scenario: your e collar is set on the right level; your dog is on a leash but a free walk meaning not at your side. Your dog spots another dog across the street. Action: give your dog his recall command. If he does not respond IMMEDIATELY, tap the e collar. It should be high enough that he comes quickly since he now understands the stimulation well. Mark and reward that response. Usually the dog will not test you more than once or twice if done correctly. Practice this ALOT.

A good way to know if your dog understands the e collar completely, while on a free walk, just tap-tap-tap the e collar. If the dog has been conditioned properly he will come to a heel position without any commands being used, I promise. Reward that behavior.

MAINTENANCE PHASE

The maintenance phase, yes, you've made it. You put in the work and the time to teach your dog a whole new language. An awesome language that will provide off leash freedom for you and your dog. After all isn't that what every dog owner wants? A well-behaved dog on and off leash at home and away from home. If that is not what you want it should be. It makes having a dog a beautiful experience. The amount of time it takes to get to this phase varies. With my own dogs, I have reached the maintenance phase in less than a week, but please remember I already have well trained dogs so it is extremely easy to teach them the meaning of the e collar. With my board and train dogs I stay in the intermittent phase for training purposes until the end of my three-week program. This way when I give the dog back to the owners they do not have to do any of the work. With that being said, I take plenty of time to teach the owners everything they need to know. With private session clients, I also have the client practice in the intermittent phase for several weeks at least. It is important that the owners and dogs get plenty of practice and repetitions for the best possible results before they are in the maintenance phase.

The maintenance phase simply means that the teaching has been done. Not that the teaching <u>IS</u> done but you put in all the work and now your dog has a full understanding of the e collar stimulation. At this stage, your dog is e collar trained and off leash reliable. The e collar is on if you go out in public and you plan on having your dog off leash. I do not need an e collar on any of my dogs when off leash in public, but I always will. Again, you have to prepare for <u>WHAT IF</u>. Dogs are not perfect. They make mistakes. Always be prepared. Your dog's life may depend on it someday.

THERE IS NO SUCH THING AS AN E COLLAR HEEL

Some of you may read this hoping to learn how to teach your dog behaviors with the e collar. I am sorry but you won't find that here. Remember, I do not teach anything with the e collar. I know that many still do use the e collar for this purpose. Believe me, it is not the way to go. Anyone can force a dog into positions. Why would a dog owner need to ever hire a trainer if that trainer was to just press a button and keep on doing so until the dog figured out the new command. Sorry but that is not dog training. I think this paragraph may ruffle many feathers but I really don't mind. The whole purpose behind me writing this handbook is to show people the proper way the tool should be used and all the benefits it can provide for anyone willing to take the time to educate their self. Remember folks we want to keep the right to use this and all tools.

I mentioned several times up until this point and probably will do so a few more times before the end that I teach everything through motivation, and positive reinforcement. I use the e collar to reinforce known behaviors, stop unwanted behaviors, make all obedience better, faster, sharper, and most of all provide off leash freedom for my dogs. It is that simple.

If you want a nice heel, teach it. Once the dog knows it well then, the e collar can be introduced to make it much better.

Take a look at the best trainers on the planet. Bart Bellon, Ivan Balabanov, and Michael Ellis are just a few. They are some of the best in the world and they are supreme motivators. They still teach through motivating dogs to the highest levels. Can any of these three stick an e collar on a dog without doing anything else and make great things happen? Yes, but you are not them.

THE MORE YOU TRAIN WITHOUT TOOLS THE BETTER THE TOOLS WORK WHEN YOU ADD THEM. TOO MUCH EMPHASIS ON TOOLS UPFRONT AND TOO LITTLE ON TEACHING.

APPLYING THE E COLLAR IN REAL WORLD BEHAVIOR PROBLEMS

Many are unsure of how to implement the e collar when faced with certain behavior problems. This can pertain to everyday dog owners or professional trainers. Aggression seems to be the subject that I am most asked about. People want to know how I use the e collar with aggression cases whether it be human or dog aggression. I have said it a thousand times before. I do not address aggression with the e collar. I do not correct or punish the aggression with the e collar, at least not on the front end. I will give a few examples to show how I use the tool in different ways on different dogs that have aggression or reactivity issues. Let me also say that over the years I have changed the way I handle truly human aggressive dogs. I say truly because I see a lot of videos of human aggressive dogs sitting next to a trainer without a muzzle and without trying to cause harm to the human. That is not true human aggression. I am talking about a dog that wants to hurt you and will try to do so very time you get close. I handle those cases from a distance now as many of you have seen from videos such as Jedi and Bear.

KEESEY THE HUMAN AGGRESSIVE PIT BULL MIX

Keesey is my most watched video. I believe I have about a quarter million views on that one video. Keesey was an extremely human aggressive dog that was scheduled to be euthanized. Several trainers attempted to work with Keesey but not a single trainer made it more than a few minutes. Once they saw what Keesey was capable of they were out. I can't blame the trainers here. Keesey was very difficult and dangerous.

What you don't see in that video is that on the day I first met Keesey he ripped his muzzle off twice and came very close to getting to me. You notice that for our first lesson he has a high-quality muzzle on. Let me also say that Keesey was the last human aggressive case that I physically handled on day one. After Keesey I started using a hands-off approach which I call **Hands Off No Conflict Aggression Rehabilitation.** Many of you have read my article or have seen me do it in videos. I much prefer the hands-off approach now. The other way was creating too much conflict and stress for both me and the dog.

With Keesey, I could not train with food because of course I could not give him my hand, and not that he would take food anyway. I used the e collar here in two very simple ways. First Keesey wanted to avoid me at all costs. He would blow up and go after me as I approached or made him come closer to me, in an attempt to back me off. This is very common with aggressive dogs. I will also say that I don't care what type of aggression we had here, it was aggression and he had intent to do harm. That is all that matters. Once I had the leash I used very gentle straight line leash pressure along with tapping the e collar on Keesey's very low working level to guide the dog toward me. Exactly what he did not want to do. Now of course he had no clue what that strange sensation of the e collar was and I think in this case it actually helped by giving him something to think about. The second Keesey moved toward me the leash pressure and the tapping of the e collar stopped. His reward was simply stopping the weird feeling but an even bigger reward was nothing bad happening when he was next to me. We did this for a short while before I quickly moved to using forward movement. I took Keesey down the street for a walk. If he attempted to nail me I just stopped him with the leash and dominant dog collar, <u>NOT THE E COLLAR</u> as so many do which would be a mistake. Once we were moving forward I started doing turnabouts tapping the e collar as I turned 180 degrees to walk the opposite direction. This taught Keesey to just follow me. Lesson two was much of the same except there was one moment that you don't see.

As Keesey's owner was taking him through the front door to meet me on the front lawn, Keesey exploded. The owner came outside. I sent her back in and made her wait at the front door. Every

15

time Keesey blew up I had her gently and smoothly pull up on the dominant dog collar controlling his neck and his breathing until he let up. Keesey literally looked at the owner as if to be in shock that she was taking control. He settled down quickly and I had her move through the doorway and come outside. It is so important that she left the house under control, which so many fail to do today. Now we could start the second lesson. Second lesson was boring and uneventful and we just repeated lesson one.

Third and final lesson I brought Bruno my Rottweiler to help. Bruno helped with all my aggression cases and it was simply amazing to watch how he worked around these dogs. To be honest, I brought Bruno to help with the training but I planned on removing the muzzle for the first time, I think part of me needed the security of knowing if Keesey latched on to me Bruno would be there. I never thought of that before until Keesey.

Something you don't see in the video is that when I went to remove the muzzle two times before the time I actually did, Bruno got a little worked up. He became very uncomfortable and he made sure I knew it. I listened to him. After a little more walking, Bruno finally acknowledged Keesey, like it was the first moment they met. That's how I knew it was time. I removed the muzzle and Keesey was beautiful. Happy and stress free and walked like a normal dog with us. The owner cried and was overjoyed. I was so happy and relieved at the same time. In the beginning I told the owners I did not know if I could do it but I would give it my best. Back then I only did 3 private sessions. I told them I would do as many sessions as I needed. It took three. The following week Keesey came to his first group class. What you get to see is not just a dog that was not trying to attack me or anyone else but a dog that was truly happy and normal. If Keesey was not trying to attack but looked beaten at the end I would consider that a failure. I have <u>NEVER</u> had a dog leave my program looking down in the dumps.

Never. If the dog looks bad by the end of a training program the training was bad. It is that simple.

Now let's make one thing very clear here. I was successful with this dog for one simple reason. THE OWNERS. They did everything I asked which included completely changing many bad habits inside the home and allowing Keesey to pretty much control everything in his life. My part was small, but their part was enormous.

One last tidbit on Keesey. I never corrected the aggression with the e collar. Through the whole process every time Keesey blew, up I took complete control of him using the leash and dominant dog collar. Now with that being said, when we were at the end of the training, if Keesey was to show signs of the aggression I could have easily stopped it before it happened with a tap of the e collar and yes it would have been higher than his working level. Not a super high level but higher. Enough to have meaning, but again I never had to. Remember what I said earlier. With good e collar work you rarely ever have to actually use it by time the training is done.

BANE THE ROTTWEILER

Bane the Rottweiler is a dog that I think many will be able to relate to. Bane came to me with his owner for private sessions not long ago. I have a video of Bane's first session on my YouTube page. Bane was a typical young Rottweiler. Stepped out of his owner's jeep and was anxious right from the start. He never really paid attention to me or his owner. He just pulled from spot to spot like a lot of young dogs do.

I had his owner take Bane by a few place boards I had laid out for that training session. I had Bane's owner walk him over to the place boards and requested that he place Bane up on the place board. Bane was very suspicious of the boards and refused to step on any of them. Next I had the owner walk Bane through some basic obedience commands. Bane really didn't do anything and was not engaging with his owner.

We spent the next thirty minutes teaching a marker word, working on engagement (eye contact), and started conditioning to the e collar. Within about that first thirty minutes I filmed Bane working with his owner. He was already starting to pay attention and he was executing some of the basic obedience commands nicely. Bane also was doing very well with his introduction to the e collar. As far as the place boards go, I never attempted to get Bane on the boards again during that session. I could have very easily forced Bane on the boards, but that would never produce the dog that I want. Bane had a tremendous fear of the boards. I mean truly petrified, not being defiant as many would label the behavior. If I were to force Bane onto the boards that would have been to feed my ego, not build Bane into the dog I need him to be.

As I do with all my clients, I gave Bane's owner very simple instructions on what to do for the next week. He was to work on engagement and continue to condition Bane to the e collar.

Within the first couple of weeks Bane's owner started sending me videos of Bane. It was awesome. Bane's obedience looked great, he was fully engaged with his owner, he was not only getting on place boards without any issues but he was also jumping in the back of his owner's jeep, and best of all Bane was working off leash out in public. Bane's owner is a rock star and put in the work and made it a point to learn what I was teaching. He even started adding in a little bite work for Bane which Bane really enjoyed.

Let's move forward to the common problems I mentioned earlier. Many of you will relate to this. Bane started becoming very reactive to other dogs while on leash. Anyone that has ever handled a worked-up Rottweiler knows how incredibly difficult it can be to take control of these powerful beasts. Bane has a female dog friend that he plays with. Other than that, he has never been around other dogs except once when he was 5 months old and that was a bad experience. The adult dog went after Bane and tried to attack him. Not what you want for your 5-month-old puppy. Now there is no way to know if that one incident is what created the issue, or if a lack of experiencing other dogs early on, or a combination of both is what created the issue of the reactivity, but it doesn't really matter. The reactivity is there.

I had the owner come back for another private session. Actually, this was the week I am writing this so very recent. I pointed out many little things that I needed the owner to change. The little decisions that the dog makes that many don't notice or pay attention to. The moving about while we are talking, the sniffing everything, the peeing when not being released. Just a few examples of the things that need to be controlled before we address the big issues. Just about every client I meet with a dog with behavioral issues allow the little things that I do not want a dog to do. THE TRAINING STARTS BEFORE THE TRAINING STARTS. Take care of the little things and the big things will take care of themselves.

After taking control of Bane we started the lesson. First, we worked on the basic obedience commands: come, sit, down, place. I had the owner use the e collar in the intermittent phase and since Bane has been at this for a while the rewards were far apart. I also had the owner keep the e collar a little higher than usual. Simply because Bane is at a point to where he knows this stuff well. He needs to know now that he does not have a choice. He must comply. Also, we are not using the e collar before the command anymore at this point, only after. Bane tested us a few times, but we just did not allow any monkey business. Once Bane settled down it was time to move onto engagement.

Bane was performing the commands but he was not dialed in to us. He was just looking everywhere else and keeping his back to us. That is definitely unacceptable and not what I want. I put Bane up high on the top of a plastic crate. I controlled him with a leash. I worked on eye contact for a few minutes using food as a reward, but no e collar use yet. After a few minutes, he was catching on. I added a LOOK command to the behavior. Now at times I would reward the second he made eye contact and sometimes I would make him hold the eye contact before rewarding. If he looked away before it was time I said Uh-Uh and gave a little leash pop. The second he looked back I rewarded.

Now it's time to add the e collar. I repeated just what I was doing as mentioned above, except this time when he looked away I tapped the e collar. At first the e collar was set at a pretty high level, up in the fifties. The reason for doing that is Bane knows what is expected here. He knew this command prior to our lesson. I was just refreshing it for him. Now the first time he looked away when I wanted him to hold the eye contact I tapped the e collar one time, he looked at me quickly and I rewarded. It is important to remember that I am not using the e collar to get him to look at me but instead I am correcting him for looking away. After the first e collar tap I moved the level of the collar into the 20s. One more correction for looking away and I was able to move the e collar back to single digits and Bane was now doing great. I stopped as soon as he was nailing it.

Next, we moved onto some bite work. Now I wanted to reward Bane for his work in the previous exercise but I also wanted to show Bane's owner what I did to improve his biting and fighting on the bite wedge. I let Bane's owner go first then I pointed out the things to change to make the game better.

I took the bite wedge and put in a little work. To keep this short Bane went from being hesitant to bite, and barely gripping to biting with a full grip, and fighting the crap out of me. That is all I wanted. I just wanted to bring the best out of Bane.

Now it was time to address the reactivity. I had Bane and his owner wait at the end of my driveway. I brought Luca out on a leash. When Luca is on leash he understands that means it is time to relax. I instructed Bane's owner to start walking down the street. Bane was staring at Luca with that typical very serious Rottweiler look. We had Bane's e collar set to the appropriate level to correct Bane for any unwanted behavior. Not crazy high, just enough to let him know his behavior was unacceptable.

As the two were walking down the street I was behind with Luca about 90 feet. I instructed Bane's owner to tap the e collar when I said to. His job was to just keep moving forward. Bane looked back at us and I had his owner tap the e collar which caused Bane to quickly look forward again walking nicely with his owner. We repeated this as needed about three times.

Next, I came up alongside of Bane and his owner. The four of us were walking nicely together and Bane was very relaxed. We came to an open field where I took Luca off leash and allowed him to go to the bathroom and run free. Then I proceeded to work Luca a little. You guys know how worked up he gets. I needed him to do that to see if we got a reaction out of Bane. We did not. Bane did great. The act of correcting Bane quickly when he was looking behind him at Luca was enough to make it very clear that that behavior would not be accepted. Let me make one other point here. I would not mind if Bane was looking at Luca. In fact, I want him to. I don't want to create avoidance. I want to create a neutral acceptance. The problem isn't looking it is fixating. Fixating is not allowed. I put Luca back on leash and we walked back to my house. Again, Bane did fantastic. This is where it gets interesting.

We stood next to my client's jeep and just talked for a while. I had Luca still on leash and he had Bane. This is an important part of the process again that many overlook. When you can interact with another person, just carry a normal conversation, the client tends to relax and take their mind off of their dog. This also allows the dog to relax because the owner is relaxed. I told my client to just do nothing to Bane. Don't give any commands and allow the dog to be with you but I also made it a point to tell the client that Bane is not allowed to move forward. Bane must just be with you. I also told the client to always be prepared for Bane to make a mistake. Guess what, as relaxed as Bane was he decided to take a quick leap forward attempting to get Luca. My client reacted perfectly and implemented a firm e collar correction. Bane retreated back to where he started. After a minute Bane laid down, which was a perfect sign and relaxed for real this time. This is where we ended our session. Everything we have done up until this point has prepared my client for WHAT IF, but also has prepared Bane to be held accountable for any unwanted behavior without any negative blow back from doing so. In fact, it just made the relationship stronger.

CORRECTIONS HAVE MUCH MORE MEANING WHEN THE RELATIONSHIP IS ALREADY THERE.

Now we will start working Bane around more dogs and more distractions. Knowing how dedicated his owner is, I know Bane will be completely fine with strange dogs in no time.

MY WORST FIRST LESSON

Not all dogs are going to be easy. Not all dogs are going to comply with what you want as an owner or trainer. Every now and then you will get a dog that makes you feel that you have very little ability as a trainer. Moose was that dog for me.

About ten years ago I was called to start working with a big beautiful lab that was adopted from a shelter. The owner lived in a busy area of Nashville, Tennessee and he really wanted to get Moose trained properly. Moose was about two years old and absolutely gorgeous. A big athletic looking Yellow Lab full of personality.

We took Moose outside and started training after spending a little time in the man's home discussing what can be expected from my training program.

I had a long line on Moose, an e collar, and a flat buckle collar. I had high value treats and was planning on using all of it in the first training session.

Let's just say Moose had different plans. The first 30 to 40 minutes was absolutely terrible. I had never been made to look so bad before by any dog in all my years of training. It was so bad at one point that I stopped and looked at the owner and said, "I swear I am actually really good at this, usually". It was bad. Moose was absolutely psychotic. I could not get him to even know I was there. He pulled and bucked and noticed everything around except for me. Before any of you ask, believe me the answer is yes. I tried everything. I did everything. Nothing came even close to working.

It was hot and I was drenched with sweat and Moose was still going strong. What I did next I never had to do before or since.

I put the e collar on a higher level that I would normally ever have to at this stage of the training. Moose was just that type of dog that was so focused on everything around him that the lowest working level he felt would have been way too high for most dogs. I tapped the button one time. If Moose reacted poorly to the higher-level stimulation I would have not continued, but in reality, this was Moose's lowest level that he felt. Moose reacted but not like a dog that was just tapped on a high level on the e collar. He barely noticed it, but at least he noticed something. I finally got his attention. He looked a little confused but he responded to me. I started the normal e collar conditioning process. I used the e collar at the higher level two times before moving the level in half. I continued to condition the dog a couple more minutes on this level but not the higher level like we started. Moose actually looked like he was enjoying the process. Within a few minutes of work I had Moose working on normal starting levels, single digits and he was responding beautifully. We ended on a good note and Moose looked good. He was still very wacky and straight up nuts.

I included this lesson because I feel it is important for all trainers, especially young trainers starting out to understand that there will be dogs that make you question your ability. These dogs will make you better. These dogs will test you and force you to step outside your comfort zone. Everything I did with Moose was in front of his owner. I will never do anything to a dog that I would not do in front of an owner, and sometimes there will be conflict. You must just work through it. It will get better. Moose is a fairly rare type of dog, but there are more like him out there. Be prepared to try something different if necessary. Without the e collar to assist me I really believe Moose would have wound up back in the shelter very quickly.

E COLLAR TRAINING
FOR FEARFUL DOGS

I know many seasoned trainers will agree with me here. Good e collar training with fearful dogs works wonders. Why, I really am not exactly sure, but trust me it does. Not only does it work wonders but it works fast. Fearful dogs are my favorite cases to work with. They are difficult and must be handled properly. At the same time, I find nothing more rewarding than taking a very timid dog with zero confidence and making it a happy confident dog. I love that feeling. I don't know the reason or science behind the remarkable results with e collars and fearful dogs, but it works. It really works. If I had to guess I would say that giving this type of dog something that it could control, the e collar stims on and off just brings out that confidence. Again, that is just my guess. I do not train any differently as far as the e collar goes with these cases. If possible just be sure to use a lot of movement and enthusiasm and getting these dogs up high on objects works wonders. Get them up high and it is difficult for them to keep their head down.

ACT OF GOD CORRECTIONS

Act of God corrections refer to corrections implemented at a very high level to stop a behavior fast many times without being associated with the handler. Think of an underground fence. Underground fences whether you like them or not work. They work because the first time the dog attempts to go past the designated boundaries it receives an Act of God correction from the e collar that is programed to the underground wire. Usually the dog never attempts to pass the boundary again. Usually but of course there are always exceptions. Once this happens to a dog the dog becomes suspicious of the area that is usually marked with flags in the beginning when the dog is learning the boundary.

Something I never do when introducing a dog to the e collar is give corrections with the tool before the dog fully understands what the stimulation means. I have used this tool every way possible over the years and have seen very experienced trainers use it every way possible and I can promise you that you will get results doing that but not the results that a good training program is capable of. When I give that first correction with the e collar whether it be a high level or low level correction I want the dog to accept it and move on like nothing ever happened.

With that been said, there are some bad behaviors that you want to correct on high levels and not be associated with you the handler.

For example, counter surfing, digging, chewing and fence jumping are just a few. These types of behaviors are best to set the dog up so you could see him but he can't see you. Once the dog is conditioned to the e collar you can stop these behaviors usually with one good correction, like the underground fence.

If counter surfing is the issue, put a plate of food on the counter where your dog usually commits the offense. Get to a place such as outside where a window provides you a good view of the food on the counter. As soon as your dog goes up to get the food give him a correction on the highest level possible. I would probably wait until the front paws hit the counter so he makes a good connection. Chances are you will never have to do it again. You have just created suspicion of the counter that will benefit you. Set up the same scenario with any of the above behaviors. Once or twice is usually all it takes. Like I said I would only do this once the dog is conditioned but I am not saying this would not work if there was no training at all yet done. If you plan on using the e collar for your dog on a regular basis condition first. If you are only wanting to stop those types of behaviors you may have success but I prefer conditioning first always.

TEACHING CLIENTS PROPER E COLLAR USE

This is crucial for all my trainers out there. Teaching our clients how to use the tool properly is extremely important. I made a video a few years ago using my daughter as the client. Essentially what I do with all clients is have them hold the e collar in their hand. I search for the lowest level possible that they can feel it, just like we do with the dogs. Once they feel something I instruct them not to move the e collar in their hand at all because just like on the dogs you will feel it differently on different parts of the hand. It may feel stronger or you may not feel it at all. Then we begin the role playing. I show them exactly what we do when we start conditioning the dog. I want them to feel the timing between the command, leash pressure, marker and of course e collar stimulation. Once the client starts to understand I put the e collar in my hand. I become the dog. I comply at first but then I start to add a little noncompliance. Things that they may experience with their dog. I teach them how to work through it. Once they are responding correctly and using proper timing, then and only then do I allow them to work the dog.

I have been doing this for many years. People just get it very fast this way. There was a time where I stopped for a little while because I find it so silly but what I realized was people really had a much harder time understanding the proper mechanics of the e collar. Also, this way allows the client to make the mistakes on me, not the dog.

ANSWERS TO COMMON E COLLAR QUESTIONS

Q. My dog does great with the e collar on leash but as soon as he is off leash he blows me off. Why?

A. This is very common and usually means a couple of things. First most people are way too quick to get rid of the leash. If your dog is blowing you off he is not ready. Use a very long line like a 30-foot line and practice in new places around real distractions. Once the dog is recalling every time no matter what, then and only then is he ready to be off leash. Also, if he is blowing you off chances are the dog does not understand as much as you think. It takes a lot of repetitions and practice before a dog truly gets it. Don't be too quick and ask for too much or you will just find yourself constantly correcting unwanted behavior. One last thing here. Many make the mistake of going out in public with the e collar set way too low. Make sure it is already set on the appropriate level before you need to use it or you will find that you are missing great opportunities to stop unwanted behavior with good timing if you have to search for the correct level.

Q. How often should my dog wear the e collar?

A. As long as you are with the dog, especially during the early stages of training have the collar on. You never want to put it on, start training right away and then take it off when you're done training. If you are going to have it on for several hours move the e collar to another part of the neck to avoid irritation from having it on one spot too long. Take it off if you leave the house and the dog is staying home. Take it off at night to sleep.

Q. What do I do if the dog won't leave my side while conditioning?

A. Many dogs will do this. We call this velcro dog. Not a problem. You do not need the dog to be far away to start conditioning with the recall. If the dog is right in front of you just take a step back as you give the recall command and utilize the e collar. Same thing if the dog is right next to you. Use small movements. Just make sure to give the command and use the e collar before the dog tries to follow your movements. When possible back up toward the dog's butt. This will cause him to turn and move toward you. Also, you can do the turnabout movements like we talked about earlier. Also, while walking forward use your momentum to get the dog going forward also and in one quick movement step back quickly. This will cause the dog to move forward without you giving you some space to call him back. I have had a few working dogs including my own that never take their eyes off of you and won't leave your side. For this type of dog teach the place command first. This way you can use the place to create distance and call the dog from the place.

Q. What if my dog won't come to me during the conditioning phase.

A. This is why it is important to utilize the leash through the process. Don't get rid of the leash until the dog is ready and that can take a little time. The last thing you want is to start correcting your dog on high levels because he won't come to you. So many make this mistake. Use the leash. Don't give your dog a chance to blow you off.

Q. What do you teach with the e collar?

A. NOTHING. Teach with motivation and positive reinforcement

Q. Can I stop unwanted behaviors with the e collar?

A. Absolutely. Where many go wrong here is they purchase an e collar, put it on the dog, and then correct or punish the dog for the unwanted behavior. I would never do that. Always condition the dog properly first. Then once the dog is trained to the e collar stopping unwanted behaviors is a breeze. In fact, there is no easier way in my opinion.

Q. Will my dog have to wear the collar forever?

A. Why wouldn't you want him to? This question is a sign to me that you see the e collar as a negative thing. It is a fabulous tool that provides off leash freedom for your dog. So, tell me why you would not want him to wear it forever. My dogs do not need an e collar on. Never. It does not matter where we are. They listen without it but if I am going to have my dogs off leash in public I am going to have an e collar on for that WHAT IF moment. You just never know.

Q. At what age do you start the e collar training?

A. I prefer the dog to be 7 or 8 months old. I have done several at 5 months old and never had a problem. I know many that start at 12 weeks old but I am not a big fan of that. At that age, I prefer to do a lot of work with food and toys.

Q. What do I do if I make a mistake?

A. You will make a mistake. You will make many. It is ok, don't worry about it. You are not a dog trainer and it can be quite difficult in the beginning even though it looks very easy. Just continue to do what you should be doing. If you do make a mistake such as hitting the button on a high level by accident and making the dog yelp, don't make a big reaction to it. Go back down to the correct level and continue working and rewarding.

Q. When and how much should I dial up levels when the dog is not responding while off leash.

A. I don't dial up levels. I always have the e collar set on the appropriate level for the situation. Also, if the dog is not responding to lower levels he is probably not ready to be off leash

Q. Does breed or size of dog make a difference on how they feel the e collar.

A. No, not at all. All dogs respond differently but breed and size does not matter. Several years ago, I was working with a Turkish Kangal. Easily the most ferocious and powerful dog on the planet. Believe me I know from experience and no I cannot share unfortunately. These dogs are flock guarding dogs and are responsible for protecting livestock from such powerful hunters like bears, wolves, and cheetahs. They make our most powerful Pit Bulls and Rottweilers look like foo-foo dogs. The Kangal I was training had already killed multiple dogs including the owners Pit Bull. I was concerned that the e collar would have absolutely no effect on a dog that could take on some pretty serious wild animals. Well I was very wrong. On low single digits the dog looked like it was going to jump in my lap. I was really blown away. At the same time, I was training a little Bichon Frise that worked on very high levels and never flinched. I learned at that time that breed and size had no impact on reaction to the e collar.

Q. Can I use the e collar to correct reactivity toward other dogs when out on walks?

A. Absolutely, if you condition the dog properly and teach like we have talked about. Please don't look for the shortcut here. So many dog owners deal with this unwanted behavior and never get it under control. This is an easy fix once the dog is conditioned, and that does not take long.

Q. Can I use it to stop barking and whining especially in the crate or car?

A. Again, of course. Just follow what I said above. You will stop it very fast. Effortless.

Q. Can you use an e collar if your dog has already been trained with an underground fence.

A. Yes, you can. In the part of the country I live in underground fences are very popular. I train many dogs that have underground fences. I don't do anything different. The only thing that changes is during the conditioning phase when searching for the dog's working level, just about every dog has the same exact reaction when they first feel the e collar. They freeze. They are scared to move. They don't want to get blasted with the underground fence. Great thing about dogs is they move on very fast. As soon as they see nothing bad happens and the rewards start coming they catch on. Start away from the home if the dog is too preoccupied on what may happen due to the fence.

Q. My dog looks depressed since my trainer started using an e collar. Is this normal?

A. Unfortunately, yes. Not because e collars should make a dog look depressed or down but because there are still a ton of trainers out there that have absolutely no business using this tool. That is not an opinion. It is a fact. A large percentage of the dogs I train have been to at least one other trainer. I can almost guarantee that if they used an e collar it was to correct and punish the dog for not complying. That's not dog training. That's abuse

Q. I have seen you and others use two receivers on the dog. Is that for more power?

A. No it is not for more power. Two receivers are used to make better contact and distribute the stim evenly on both sides of the neck. With some dogs, it can be difficult to keep the collar from moving and becoming loose. Two receivers, one on each side will usually help and also allow you to keep the strap not as tight as a single receiver set up.

Q. Do you use the vibration button?

A. No I do not. Here is why. Many people tell me their dog responds to the vibration while off leash every time. They recall to the vibration without any problems. That is fine, but what happens when they don't? If the dog is not trained to the e collar stimulation you can't turn to it when your dog decides to chase a deer instead of responding to the vibration. It is just not fair and also it may cause the dog to run away faster not knowing what the stimulation is. There has to be a consequence for not responding, especially when the situation can put your dog in harm's way. The dog must be conditioned and trained to the stimulation if you plan on having your dog off leash. Also, if you are so set on using only the vibration most likely you still see this tool as a negative thing which means you should not use it.

On the other hand, now there are adjustable vibration only collars that can be purchased. I know E Collar Technologies is making one that people like very much. An adjustable vibration only collar would be fine if you plan on keeping your dog on leash. It can also serve a purpose inside the home for people that are dead set against full blown e collar training. I don't have a problem with that, but again if your dog is going to be off leash in public please use true e collar training.

MAKING GOOD CONTACT WITH THE E COLLAR

Making good consistent contact with the e collar is one of the biggest problems we have as e collar users. One of the biggest mistakes I see is people putting the collar on way too loose. In order to make good consistent contact the collar must be very snug so the contact points make contact to the skin. You should never be able to move the collar around without loosening it.

Let's discuss a few tips to help with better contact. First make sure the dog's neck is brushed out very well. Dead hair will prevent good contact. When putting the collar on have the dog in a down or stand position. This puts the dog's neck in a good neutral position making it easy for a true fit on the neck. When the dog is sitting in front of you they tend to look up or down putting the neck in a bad position for true e collar fitting. As soon as the neck goes to a true neutral position the collar comes loose.

Place the collar high on the neck off to one side or the other. Placing the collar higher up behind the ear helps with dogs that have long hair or loose skin. Once you pull the straight end of the collar strap through the buckle loop be sure to take your finger and pull the dog's hair out from the buckle. Pull all the hair out or you will think you have a tight fit when in reality the hair is preventing good snug contact. Many times, when you get the collar buckled and the dog relaxes his neck you will have to go back and make it one or two holes tighter. When fitted properly you should barely be able to get two fingers under the collar strap on top of the neck.

Also, be sure to use the appropriate length contact points. Short hair dogs can use short contact points. Longer hair dogs may need longer contact points. Don't assume that using the longest contact points will make for better contact. Very long points can cause the receiver to be pushed on its side when tightened properly. The longer points can push the receiver to a poor position and that is not what we want.

CONDITIONING THE DOG IN BUSY PLACES

Not everyone lives in the suburbs or on a farm. A lot of trainers and dog enthusiasts that I speak to on daily basis live in very busy places like New York City or Mumbai, India. Sometimes it is not feasible to find a place with no distractions to condition the dog as we normally do. In this case we have a couple of options.

First option is we can condition the dog outdoors in an area with the least amount of distractions possible. I know that may still be a very busy area but that is ok. You will condition the dog as we always do. The only difference here is that the dog's lowest working level perceived most likely will be higher than a dog that is conditioned without distractions around. That is totally fine, it is not a problem. The lowest level perceived is the lowest level perceived. Once you find the lowest working level it is possible that once the conditioning starts you may have to go lower on the levels because the dog many times will become more sensitive to the stimulation once they make a connection with what is going on. Remember we always want the lowest level felt during the teaching.

Another option is to condition your dog inside the home. Of course, you may not be able to use a longer leash and the dog may not be able to move very far from you but again this is ok. We are only wanting to start conditioning the dog to that weird sensation that is completely foreign to the dog. The problem with this is that if you do decide to work outside you will have to adjust the levels anyway so why not just start outdoors where it is busy. I would start the conditioning outside where it is busy and you can always practice indoors after the fact on the dog's true lowest level perceived.

Both options are fine and if you condition the dog properly, fairly, and humanely you will end up at the desired destination. A well trained off leash dog that understands the e collar as a beautiful language that provides freedom and options.

FIXING A DOG THAT HAS BEEN THROUGH BAD E COLLAR TRAINING

A few years back I met with a woman at her home to work with her female Pitbull. The dog had aggression issues toward other dogs. The woman informed me that she had recently spent $4700 at another Nashville trainer only to have the dog come back worse than she was before. I knew the trainer. I knew this trainer had no ability to work with difficult dogs, and I also knew that this trainer had no ability with the e collar. In fact, this trainer had destroyed many dogs with the e collar that I would end up with at my home. I eventually worked with this trainer after he asked for help. I did not charge. It was important to me that the misuse of the e collar stopped and that the harsh tactics on the dogs he was training also stopped.

We sat down and discussed what the woman's expectations were for her dog. She made it very clear that she did not want to use an e collar. When I asked why she told me about the problems with the other trainer I just mentioned above. I said no problem. I never push anyone toward e collar training if they don't want it but once they see how I use it they always decide to add the e collar to the training.

This client was no different. We had a great first lesson. The second lesson the client says to me she wants to give the e collar another shot. When I asked why she said after seeing how I handled her dog, seeing what my dogs look like, and meeting a few of my clients in the neighborhood she was comfortable with me doing so. She asked if I could fix the problems the last trainer created with the abusive e collar work. I said absolutely. I do it all the time.

She asked me to show her how the dog would respond to it after having a very bad experience. This dog already trusted me and was working well with me because of the work we did at the first lesson. I put the e collar on the dog and we started. The dog worked on a number 2 on a collar with 100 levels. Very sensitive as many dogs are. At first, when she felt it she froze like a dog that is trained with an underground fence. She did not have experience with an underground fence but did have experience in getting blasted on high levels. I worked as I do any other dog. At first, she would not take food as a reward but that changed after 5 minutes. The dog looked great and was moving about beautifully. She almost seemed relieved that nothing bad happened. I stopped after a few minutes to instruct the owner as I always do, except I usually do that first.

We started the role playing. The owner held the collar and I started teaching her just like we have discussed. She was surprised by how light the stimulation was. After she was understanding the timing and the mechanics I placed the receiver in my hand. She searched for my level. I did not feel the stimulation until the collar was in the high 30's. She practiced on me. She made some mistakes with the timing as most do but we worked through it. I became less compliant as the dog and once the client was responding properly it was time to put the e collar back on the dog.

I walked her through the process. She gave the Come command, guided the dog with the leash as she tapped the e collar right after the command. The dog yelped loudly. We realized that the remote was left on the high 30's from when she was working me. The woman was devastated and get upset. I took her by the arm, looked her straight in the eye, and said it's ok, watch me. I took the dog and put the e collar back on a 2. The dog went right back to normal and was still taking food. <u>The terrible mistake was not that terrible</u>. Even though this dog had been through bad e collar training she recovered from just a few minutes of proper training.

This case is a perfect example of how all dogs respond that have had bad experiences with the e collar. I work with many dogs that have been through the same situation. They all come around and come around fast. I do not do anything different. I treat every dog with care and compassion and work on building the dog up, not breaking them down.

You also saw that we made a big mistake here. It is my mistake not the client's. I should have double checked but I did not. **You will make mistakes**. We all do. Don't dwell on it, just move forward and everything will be alright.

USING THE E COLLAR FOR ADVANCED OBEDIENCE

There are no limits to how you can improve your overall training program if the conditioning has been done properly. I know you are probably sick of hearing that by now but it is that simple. Take the time to teach the dog the meaning of the e collar stimulation and you can implement the tool to stop the things you don't like and make the things the dog knows better, faster, and sharper under all circumstances. It is that easy.

I have worked with countless competitors from different dog sport backgrounds. Many of them have been successful for a long time and have avoided e collars because when they started in their sport, e collars were mostly used for punishment. Unfortunately, many still think like that. Once these competitors learn the conditioning process, they are able to elevate their dogs even higher than they were before. There is always room for improvement. In many cases, it just takes the addition of the e collar to add that little something that was missing before. No other tool can provide that.

Teaching the e collar to a high level gives you that ability to communicate with your dog from a distance even with the highest level of distractions, and still hold the dog accountable when compliance is not met. For example, let's say I am working one of my dogs from a distance. We are practicing positions, Sit, Down, Stand, and Reverse. As I am calling out the different commands while my dog is in a down, I give the Stand command. The dog does not perform the Stand command immediately. I tap the e collar right after I see that the dog did not comply and the dog will pop right up into a stand every time without repeating the command. If the dog is trained properly they will always revert back to the last command given. The e collar tap is not delivered at a high and punitive level but rather the dog's working level in that environment. It is a reminder that says I asked you to do this, you know this well, and you must do it. No other tool can provide that.

A FEW QUICK REMINDER TIPS

1. Teach everything through motivation and positive reinforcement.

2. Build the relationship and earn the trust.

3. Condition the dog properly before ever using it for corrections.

4. Teach the dog the language and take your time.

5. Dogs learn through repetitions not duration. Keep the sessions short, 5 to 10 minutes a few times a day.

6. Keep the dog's neck brushed well to make good contact.

7. Make sure the collar fits snug and does not move.

8. Never attach the leash to the e collar.

9. Find the appropriate working level without distractions present when possible.

10. Use food to reward during the early training.

11. Do not get rid of the leash prematurely.

12. Never give the dog a chance to blow you off during the training. Keep the leash there to prevent this.

13. Cheat if you must, meaning make it simple for the dog. Set them up to succeed, not fail.

14. Keep the e collar on the dog if you are with them.

15. Move the collar on the neck if it will be worn for several hours to avoid irritation.

16. Take it off at night to sleep and keep the collar charged.

17. Practice everywhere you can.

18. Plan on training with the e collar for at least a few months to truly teach the dog the language fluently.

19. Most of all enjoy the process. The more you do with your dog the better the relationship becomes. The better the relationship becomes the more the dog will learn from you. Repetitions build competence, competence builds confidence.

TRAINING TIPS FOR ANY TYPE OF TRAINING

1. **Be in charge but also build the relationship**. Structure is very important during the early stages of training. You must provide the guidance your dog needs to learn how to thrive and succeed in the household with the family. Rules and boundaries are very important and must be consistent but so is building a strong bond and relationship. Your dog is exactly that, a dog, not a child. **Treat your dog like a child and your dog will treat you like a dog. It just does not work**

2. **Reward good behavior.** When your dog does something right, let him know. If you want to give affection, do so when your dog is in the right state of mind, calm and relaxed, not when he or she is excited or demanding attention. Paying attention or giving affection when your dog is not behaving properly only encourages bad behavior.

3. **Correct unwanted behavior.** If your dog does something wrong 100 times and you correct it 99 times they will continue to take that chance. You must correct unwanted behavior every time or your dog will not stop that behavior.

4. **Show your dog what you want.** It is not fair to just expect your dog to understand what you want. You must show her and show her clearly what you are asking.

5. **Motivate your dog to do what you want.** Once you show your dog what you want, then you must motivate him or her to do so, with food, or toys, or praise. Whatever works to get the dog excited and willing to learn is what you need to use.

6. **Make your dog do it.** Once you have shown your dog what you want and the dog 100% understands the command, then and only then can you make your dog perform that com-

mand. It is not fair to try to make a dog do something when he or she does not have a full understanding of what you are asking. On the other hand, when your dog truly understands what you are asking, then the dog must do what you ask.

Dogs do not understand people psychology, so do not try to put human thoughts in your dog's head. You will not hurt your dog's feelings by taking charge and providing consistency with rules and boundaries. In fact, they will love and respect you even more for it because now they can put their trust in you as their leader and you remove that stress from them.

Make your dog wait at every doorway during the training process going out and in. I do not care if my dogs run out the door when we go outside but my dogs are already trained. When they were young and in the training process I practice this a lot. It goes a long way.

Keep training short, no more than 10 or 15 minutes at a time. You could do this a few times a day and it could be done in your home. You do not want them to get bored. Keep it fun and incorporate play with training. When you stop, your dog should want to keep working. This helps keep the dog wanting to work. Make your dog work for his food. Instead of just putting the bowl down give a few commands first, then reward with the food. Dog training is very simple, remember....

Be In Charge and Build the Relationship, Reward Good Behavior, Correct Bad Behavior, Show The Dog What You Want, Motivate It To Do So, Make The Dog Do It

MY OVERALL SUMMARY

I train dogs because I want to not because I must. I don't have to train dogs to make a living. I do it because it is my passion, it is my obsession. I am and will be a student of dog training for the rest of my life.

Over the years, I have seen the level of dog training improve a great deal. Training has become easier on the dogs, more pleasant for the dogs, and the results are better than ever for those that commit to improving.

Young trainers have the internet, social media, and YouTube at their fingertips where they can watch and learn from whereas years ago you had to figure it out the hard way. Many mistakes can be avoided today thanks to all the information available.

With that being, said there is still plenty of bad information out there. It is up to you to see through the bad and seek out the good. Are the people you look to putting out beautiful work or are you falling for the **Used Car Salesman Pitch**.

The dog is the proof. Dogs don't lie. The beautiful thing about dogs is that they change the minute we change. They are not like us. They are better. No Hang ups.

Treat the animal with respect and compassion. Treat the owner with the same if you are a trainer and give them everything you have. Be honest. Don't hide anything. If you would not do it in front of the client don't do it behind their back.

This book is on the proper use of the e collar. It is an incredible tool when in the right hands, but it is still just a tool. You must be able to train to a high level without tools. Reach this and when you do add tools they are that much more effective.

First and foremost, you must develop the relationship and have the trust from the dog. This does not take long. Again, dogs change instantly. Take advantage of that. **TRAINING STARTS BEFORE THE TRAINING STARTS. THE SECOND YOU TAKE THAT LEASH YOU ARE SPEAKING TO THE DOG. NOT WITH WORDS BUT WITH YOUR INTENTIONS. DOGS GET IT. THEY DON'T SPEAK PEOPLE, THEY SPEAK DOG.**

Learn to speak through the leash. This is 100% necessary for high level training. Learn leash pressure, gentle straight line leash pressure. Once you do this any tool you choose to use will work as it is meant to. Prong, choke, and e collars all get misused when leash pressure is not understood. Proper leash work allows these tools to work the way they were meant to, with very little effort and conflict and humanely.

Teach everything through motivation and positive reinforcement. Those that are against using food in training are just flat out missing the boat.

CLICKER AND E-COLLAR TOGETHER CREATES HARMONY

Teach behaviors through repetitions. Keep sessions short and fun. Dogs learn through repetitions not duration. Once the command is 100% understood by the dog then you can reinforce with the e collar to make better, faster, and sharper.

Stop unwanted behaviors fast. Don't make the mistake of being a nag or starting low with corrections. Start high and stop it fast. You will be able to go low very fast when done correctly. Starting low and keep going up on levels to correct will allow the dog to adapt to your nagging and take high level corrections without flinching. Don't do this.

Teach as much as you can. You could never teach too much. The more the dog knows the better and the more you teach the better the bond a relationship become.

Obedience is easy. A monkey can train a dog to do things. What you do or don't do in the home creates the dog you have, good or bad. This doesn't't take much effort. You are doing something any way, just do the right thing by your dog. I never told my wife I was going outside to train my children. We just raised them along the way. Showing them right from wrong and what was expected. It is the same thing with your dog.

Set rules and boundaries inside the home and follow them. Be consistent.

FOR ALL TRAINERS

First I would like to thank everyone that thinks enough of me as a trainer and has taken the time to read what I have written about my use of the e collar.

My goal is not only to show the proper and humane use of the tool but to also bring trainers from both sides together with a better understanding of how our dog training tools are used by responsible trainers.

Both purely positive and balanced trainers have so much good to offer to each other. I believe the best on both sides ultimately want the same thing… what is best for the dog.

The following is a comment from a video I made. It was a Rottweiler's first e collar session and this individual went to my video to make nasty remarks due to the fact she was anti e collar. This is what she said:

"This has to be the best video I have ever seen. BTW I watched wanting to hate you because I never been a fan of e collars but you won me over. Clearly whatever you are doing works and it isn't hurting the animal. I'm going to subscribe. Thanks for the humor and brutal honesty. We need more dog lovers/trainers like you".

That comment made my day the morning it popped up on my phone. Not because of the compliments but because it showed a person with a very negative view of e collars a different side, a good side. This person had a belief system that most anti e collar people have, but when shown a different way she had the intelligence and ability to see what can be. The wonderful possibilities this tool provides when in the right hands. There are many more like her and I have been lucky enough to have met and worked with a lot of them.

I have had pp trainers attack me before, but it has been rare. The ones that have come at me back off pretty quick because it is impossible to say I ever cause harm to a dog. Compassion for the animal is a priority for me and is for many balanced trainers.

Fear, force, and pain should not be part of a training program. That is not dog training. Trainers that use fear, force, and or pain to teach a dog **are not balanced trainers**, they are individuals with little or no ability to train any other way. Purely positive trainers are not wrong when they target these folks but at the same time pp trainers need to understand reputable balanced trainers are also against this type of training.

Hopefully the best on both sides can sit down someday and discuss the subject openly and honestly. I think both sides will see that we have more in common than not.

BONUS MATERIAL!

THE POWER OF THRESHOLDS

The power of working thresholds with a dog in training is a tremendously powerful tool but so often overlooked. Many trainers discount this exercise. I could not disagree more. It is one of the first things I do when starting a new dog.

It is a very simple task yet will set the tone instantly. I don't speak, I don't use commands, and I don't block the doorway. I don't care if the dog is sitting, standing or laying down, it just doesn't matter. I try to use very little leash pressure, or none if possible.

Here is what I do: I approach a closed door with the dog at my side, and I don't say anything. I open the door and when the dog starts to move forward, which they usually will, I give a little bump with my leg. Possibly give an "uh-uh" the first time which is my "no" command, but only do that once if at all. I will stand off to the side giving the dog all the room in the world to move forward. Again, if the dog attempts to move forward a give a bump of the leg. When the dog is relaxed and no longer attempting to move through the doorway I don't say anything, I don't look or wait for the dog, I just go through the doorway and the dog follows. It is that simple but tremendously powerful.

When you can get an untrained and unruly dog that is used to pulling with all its force and running through every doorway changing its usual behavior so that the dog now looks to you for guidance, without ever uttering a word, it is a beautiful thing. That connection allows the relationship and learning to begin. It speaks volumes without any words.

MY NEW FRIEND LOKI

It was a beautiful spring weekend in South Central Kentucky. Perfect weather to be outside working dogs. I took the Friday off work and my wife joined me and Luca for a fun filled training weekend at Mohawk Malinois.

Since this training was being held at Mohawk's, of course almost all the dogs there were Belgian Malinois. I do not get to train my own dogs very often so I thought this would be a great opportunity to get Luca out and exposed to all kinds of distractions while working on the things he knows. Luca really impressed Stephanie and me by not only how he performed, but by how unbelievably calm and stable he is around total chaos, because with dozens of Malinois around sometimes it is chaos. Apparently, many others were impressed also since I have received so many emails and incredibly kind words about the work that Luca and I do together. I appreciate that very much and I am humbled by it a great deal.

On the first day, I noticed a woman working a beautiful jet black German Shepherd puppy. I could tell she was trying to expose him to new things and work him around new distractions. I offered to let Luca help in the socialization and she took me up on the offer and trained her puppy up on a table with Luca sitting by his side. The puppy did fantastic and made a new friend. The owners name was Carol, a super nice lady with a tremendous love for her dogs. Carol later explained that she also had the puppy's dad with her and planned on bringing him out also to do some training.

A little while later, I looked up and saw Carol with what looked exactly like her puppy except about 60 to 70 pounds larger. A breathtaking looking jet black adult size version of her little puppy. That was Loki, her puppy's dad.

I watched as Carol worked with Loki. You can tell he was an extremely powerful dog, and although Carol is very humble, she does an amazing job with him. It was obvious that Loki liked to work and it was also obvious that Loki liked to win and would challenge the handler when playing a fun game of tug.

At one point while I was working Luca, Carol commented to me that Luca had a beautiful "out". For non-dog people that just means that Luca releases whatever he has in his mouth when I ask him to whether it is someone's arm or a tug toy. Carol said, "I wish Loki would out like that". "It is the one thing I have a hard time with". I replied that he can, it is actually very easy, to which Carol laughed and said something to the effect of yeah right. I understand where she is coming from. In the working dog world, as well as the pet dog training world you see a lot of conflict between handler and dog. The handler pushes and the dog pushes back. The handler pulls and the dog pulls back. It is a never-ending battle but it does not have to be.

Later that weekend I saw a few different people work with Loki. I did not pay much attention because I know how I am. If I see something that can be done a better way I have a hard time keeping my mouth shut. Plus, my wife reminded me several dozen times when she saw me watching something I did not like to LET IT GO. She is good like that.

Later in the day several of us were hanging around together. My kids were also there at this point so it was great family fun. Carol asked me to work Loki to which I denied her. Not because I did not want to, but because I knew I had the potential to keep him for a while and maybe not give up until he was performing like I would want him to. Carol asked again, well actually she demanded and pushed him on me in a way I could not refuse. Carol has a great personality and is just very likable so it is hard to say no to her.

 I agreed and took Loki and his tug toy. Now those that know me, know damn well that I am going to work his "out" since that is where Carol is having trouble. I let Loki bite the tug. We fought a little. We played. We battled. He stared right into my eyes with a hard look, a challenge, daring me to win. I asked Loki to out. He did not. I made the tug go dead. I had to wait a long time and Loki did not want to out. Carol was right. Now this is where most people would yell or scream or pressure Loki with a prong collar or a choker. That would just make Loki fight harder. He is a tough guy, a warrior. He will fight force with force every time and Carol will never truly have that harmony and that flow that she and Loki deserve.

Loki finally released the tug. Only after he had felt that he won the fight. Now it was time for me to show Loki a better way. I held the tug and when Loki tried to take it I very calmly looked him in the eye, shook my head, and said "uh-uh". I did not say "NO" because I am sure that many of the dogs out there thought their name was "NO". Loki backed off, looking me right in the eye, but not with a warrior look. He looked at me with a soft eye. His eyes were asking me what I wanted. Now I can begin.

Very subtlety I backed up. No leash pressure, and Loki followed. I moved to the side, and Loki followed. I moved toward him, and he backed up, all through this keeping excited eye contact, waiting in anticipation. I lightly touched his face, then his hind quarters. I spit in my hand and held his nose gently, letting him learn who I am. I don't think anyone noticed the little things. The dopamine was rising in Loki. The anticipation of what is to come makes the body release dopamine. That makes the dog work hard to get what he wants. **The anticipation is much stronger than the actual reward.**

Now we were ready to play together, not against each other. I let Loki hit the tug. I asked him to "out". He hesitated, I held his leash with one hand just as I did when I had him following me, no pressure, and outed quite quickly. The second he outed I said "yes" and he hit the tug again. This time when I gave the out command he released immediately and in doing so I rewarded him immediately. We continued our game. Loki still stared into my eyes while we were tugging but this time it was not in defiance, but with love. I just met this dog and already we were developing a relationship. As I told Carol earlier, it is easy, it really is.

Several people came up to me afterwards wanting to know why that dog outed so easily for me and I did nothing to him. See that is the problem. **I did plenty with him, not to him**. The average dog owner or dog trainer does not see or do the little things, the things that matter. Not one person noticed me touch his face when we were moving together. Not one person saw me talk to him in a very subtle way. Not a single person recognized the moment his eyes went from hard to soft while we were staring at each other. These things matter.

Force creates one of two things: More force or submission, and neither are beneficial. Relationship and engagements creates harmony.

I can't thank Carol enough for letting me play with Loki. Carol thanked me for working with him but really, I was the one that benefited. I decided to write about my short experience with Loki because I found myself thinking of him a lot. There is something about a beautiful Shepherd, that look of intelligence and confidence that gets me every time and when they give you their heart there is no better feeling as a dog handler.

I am sure that Carol and Loki will be friends with the Krohn family for a very long time.

BRUNO, THE ULTIMATE ROTTWEILER

My wife was several months pregnant with our first child. We were flying home to New Jersey early in the morning for our baby shower at my parent's house in New Jersey. Cyrus, our 6-year-old Rottweiler started crying out loudly in the middle of the night. I jumped up and realized that he could not get up from the floor. His legs were not working. We cancelled our trip and rushed Cyrus to our vet first thing in the morning. It was horrible news. He had bone cancer. We came home devastated. We decided to take him back to the vet that day to put him to sleep. There was no way we would allow him to suffer through another night. I will never forget that trip back to the vet. I was in the back of our little pick-up truck and Stephanie was driving. Cyrus held his head high with his ears blowing in the wind. It was an extremely difficult time. We held him on the floor as he fought and thrashed trying not to go to sleep. We were broken.

A few months later we decided we could not be without a Rottweiler. We started our search but could not find the right litter. We found a family in Eastern Kentucky that had a litter on the ground. This family had never bred dogs before and this was their first time. I liked what I saw in the pictures so we made the four-hour drive.

We arrived at a home far out in the country. As we parked in front of the home a Rottweiler was laying on the front steps of the home. When the dog saw us she jumped up, opened the front door on her own, disappeared for a few seconds, and ran out with a toy in her mouth to greet us. I was very impressed. She barely resembled a Rottweiler since she had 13 puppies and was sucked down to nothing, but that big Rotty personality was still there.

We met with the owners and they took out all thirteen puppies. I asked to see the dad. The man of the house was very honest in telling me that the dad was a lunatic and was hard to control around new people and the livestock that was roaming around. That concerned me a little but the momma dog made up for it.

Stephanie and I watched and interacted with all the puppies. We both decided that one was capturing both of our attention and we decided to make the drive home with him. We called him Bruno, and our lives were about to change.

We quickly realized that baby Bruno was more than a handful. In fact, he was the worst puppy we ever had. He was a lunatic, a monster, a demon. He never stopped moving, barking, biting. We asked ourselves, "what did we do"?

We brought Bruno home in May of 2005. Our first child, Sophia was born in July 2005. Here we go, now it was total chaos. A new born baby that did not sleep because she was sick and a new puppy that we believed was psychotic.

Just when we thought it could not get worse, I had to leave for 6 months of training for work. I am a Federal Agent and sometimes that happens, but the timing could not be worse.

Now my poor wife really had her hands full. There was a time when I thought that without me there we may have to get rid of Bruno. My wife being the rock star she is, was against that and really stepped up and did a tremendous job handling a new baby, a new puppy, and Ben our 3-year-old dog. Everyday Stephanie strapped a backpack to Bruno and loaded both sides with bags of rice. She would run every day, Bruno on one side, Ben on the other, and pushing Sophia in a baby stroller. That is hard core. She had to do that just to drain enough of Bruno's energy to be able to control him in the house.

Once I returned home from training I saw how much my baby and puppy had grown. We had an awesome family with a baby and two dogs. We were so happy, but it was still a lot of work.

Fast forward a couple of years and Bruno was a different dog. He was extremely driven and energetic but now we put all that energy into training and he excelled at everything we did.

At around 3 years old Bruno was helping me train dogs. He travelled with me everywhere meeting people and dogs all over the country. He loved everyone and would drop a tennis ball at a total stranger's feet just waiting for them to throw the ball.

Bruno was born in 2009 and passed in 2016, right before Sophia was born (My Daughter). He taught me more than I ever taught him. He was truly the greatest dog I've ever known. Bruno had fans all over the world. This picture is what I loved most about him. He was the ultimate friend. He will never truly be gone.

WE GO TO DENVER

When Bruno was 4 years old we traveled to Denver, Colorado together. I purchased a dog training franchise and spent a few weeks with the company to learn about the business. I knew Bruno was a special dog but I guess I did not know to what level until other dog trainers met Bruno. He was such a big hit with everything we did. Very quickly everyone realized that if we were working with an aggressive dog Bruno was the dog that we needed to help us. He had an incredible ability to provide what the troubled dog needed, making our job so much easier. It was an amazing thing to watch. I remember one morning during one of our many group classes. There was another Rottweiler that had a bad attitude. He was a little aggressive to other dogs but really hated Bruno. He would go after Bruno every chance he had and Bruno just ignored him and stayed focused on me. Then one morning I guess Bruno knew it was the right time to take-action. This same Rottweiler went into his normal tough guy bullying and Bruno just erupted. The biggest deepest bark while raising his two from legs and landing with his chest blown up with a look on his face that I had never seen. He looked right through that other Rottweiler and that big nasty Rottweiler quickly turned into a pussy cat. All the group class attendees, mostly women, let out all kinds of gasps and laughs and one woman yelled out "Bruno, I did not know you had that in you" It was awesome and the best part was that Bruno went right back to his happy stable self. The mean Rottweiler never misbehaved again.

Another great memory I have in Colorado was Bruno's first swim. He had never been in the water. Myself and a few other trainers drove up to a lake in the Rocky Mountains. A Rottweiler, two Belgian Malinois, a Black Lab and a Pitbull all crammed into one vehicle with 5 trainers. What a sight but think about the level of training of those dogs to be able to do that without any problems. Pretty impressive.

Now it was time to get Bruno in the water. He would not follow the other dogs in so I had to convince him that he could do it. I tossed his tennis ball, which he would run through a brick wall for, just a foot into the water. Just about six inches of water. Bruno retrieved the ball and came back to me. I repeated this several times each time getting him deeper into the water until he was chest deep. Then I gave the ball a good toss out far into the water. Bruno started to go after it until he sank and his head went under water. He did an about face and came back without the ball. His expression was hysterical. We sent one of the Malinois in to get Bruno's ball and once he saw that he became Michael Phelps. He swam as fast as he could, got to his ball, got out of the water and took his ball far away from the lake hiding behind a vehicle. It was priceless. I have really beautiful memories with Bruno in Colorado.

Once we returned from Colorado Bruno was my full-blown partner and right hand man. He traveled all the time with me and immediately started becoming a very important part of my success with aggression cases. He had such a calming effect on these dogs and knew just what to do and when to do it. I did not teach that, he was just being himself. Shortly after our Colorado trip I booked our first trade show. I rented a table for $60 at a gun show in Smyrna, Tennessee. I did not know what to expect and when I arrived that Saturday morning with my wife, Bruno, and baby Sophia I was devastated. It was not a Beverly Hills Boat show to say the least. In fact, when we walked in to set up I almost left. I did not want my wife and daughter to be in that environment. My wife convinced me to stay and talked me out of my negative thoughts which she does quite often to this day. That Saturday our table had people gathered around the whole time we were there. Everyone wanted to meet Bruno. He walked around liked he owned the place greeting everyone that even looked at him. That $60 investment made us over $7000 that day. That was all Bruno. Dog owners that saw him there wanted what I had. A happy and well behaved off leash dog. It was that simple. We continued to have great success at any show we did.

For the next several years Bruno continued to be a huge part of our family and the dog training world. We trained hundreds of dogs together. I watched as he aged and traveling became more difficult for him. His legs were going but he still had the love and desire to do things together. It was hard for me to leave the house to see clients and must leave him behind. I felt guilty as he would watch me knowing what I was going to do and then seeing me leave without him.

I could tell stories about him all day. There are many wonderful memories. Out of all my memories of Bruno the love and interaction he had with my kids is by far what I loved most about him. It was a beautiful thing to watch. He watched over them with so much love and care and I always knew that if he was with them I never had to worry about anything.

Fast forward to that weekend before we lost him. It was a Saturday night. I was sitting on my couch drinking a glass of whiskey. I asked my wife to take a picture of me and Bruno. I told my wife that he would not be around much longer and that thought brought great sadness to me. I know my dogs very well. I know when they are not right. I always have. I guess it comes from the strong bond that we have.

That Monday morning when I awoke I told my wife that it would be soon. Bruno was having trouble breathing. I thought he may be going into heart failure. I took him to the vet that morning. The news was devastating. His lungs were filled with cancer. We cried. We cried a lot. I am crying as I remember this. I could not imagine life without him. Stephanie and I decided to do what needed to be done at that moment. I would never let my dogs suffer, never. Our vet sedated him so he would be almost sleeping, very relaxed. I was on the ground with him, holding him and telling him how much I loved him and thanking him for everything. I though he was out when I went to stand up. He grabbed me with his paw one last time so I stayed down with him. We watched and held him as he went peacefully.

The house has not been the same since we lost him. We have all forgotten at times and have expected to be greeted when we walk in the house. It is a constant reminder, but this is the bad part of having dogs. I would not trade the time we had together for anything. We were so lucky to have the love of the greatest Rottweiler that ever lived. Thank you, Bruno, for everything. We love you always.

WHY I GIVE FREE GROUP CLASSES

Last year I gave a free group class to anyone that wanted to attend. I thought three or four people would show up. I was drastically wrong. A lot of people showed up. A lot of awesome people. That free group class turned into a five-hour mini workshop.

There was a woman from a shelter that showed up toward the end with a big beautiful Pit Bull. She told me that they can't place him in a home because he's extremely dog aggressive. I took the dog from her but kept her with me as we spoke. The training had started but she just didn't know it. Out of all the dogs there I saw that the Pit Bull was focused on a big powerful Rottweiler. I knew the Rottweiler. He's a well-balanced big beautiful Rotty with an owner that loves dogs as much as I do.

The Pit Bull was wearing a prong collar. Wrong tool for this situation. A prong collar is used to create activity in the dog. When used in this situation it can create a lot of frustration and make things worse. I'm not against prong collars. They're good tools, but just usually used incorrectly.

I asked the shelter employee to watch from the side with all the others. I asked the Rotty owner to walk toward me and listen to my instructions. As he moved forward the Pit Bull started targeting him. I instructed the Rotty owner to stop right where he was and do nothing. I did nothing. The Pit Bull was focused on him with a serious intensity. After 20 or 30 seconds the pit bull looked up at me. I instructed the Rotty owner to move away from us back to where he was at the start. Then we repeated, each time getting the Rottweiler closer.

After about 10 minutes and several repetitions, without ever uttering a single command or implementing a single correction, the Pit Bull laid down and relaxed with the Rottweiler next to us.

The shelter worker cried. Well worth a free group class. FOR ME.

MY FAVORITE TRAINING DAY AND 14 IRISH WOLFHOUNDS

It all started when I received a call from a woman about her Irish Wolfhound that was labeled aggressive. The woman told me that her vet and even the rescue the dog came from recommended that the dog be put to sleep due to his aggression issues. This lady lived in an area that I do not travel to, but I had to make an exception because I just can't handle hearing about a pet being put to sleep when I know most likely it can be fixed very easily.

When I arrived at the home I met with the woman that called me, her husband, and her two boys were there also. I was shocked to hear that the dog would not let anyone in the home deal with him except the woman that called me. We sat in the kitchen and what I saw was not an aggressive dog but rather a dog that was scared to death of everything. The opening of a cabinet would send this dog running. This dog's name was Fletch, and Fletch had a Wolfhound sister named Fiona.

During my meeting and conversation with the family Fletch remained out of the room but where he could keep an eye on me. Fiona however was up in my face and demonstrating very rude and pushy behavior even though I never acknowledged her presence as I never do when meeting new dogs. At one point Fiona became so pushy that I stood up and sent her away, not with words or corrections but just good old fashion body language and energy. Fiona got the picture and walked away and laid down like a well-behaved dog.

At that moment Fletch came into the kitchen and laid down near me without a care in the world. As I was speaking to the owners they interrupted me and said, "I can't believe what I'm seeing". I said, "what is that"? They replied that Fletch has never been able to relax around anyone but the lady of the house before. You see, what he had here was a very insecure dog, and a dog that feared everything. Fletch had no faith in his leadership. His owners loved him and he loved them but that security just was not there for him. On top of that Fletch had a sister that was rude and pushy and was running the household. By me coming in and taking over without anger, excitement, or fear, Fletch had someone that made him feel a little more comfortable. Once I stood up and put Fiona in her place, Fletch had found what he had needed for a long time. A true leader that was willing to take control of everything around him.

Now it was time to get Fletch to accept the other family members and live life like a normal dog.

For a long time the man of the house had tried the normal things that most people do when trying to greet a dog or get a dog to be your pal. The hand out, the baby talk, and the use of treats. All of this is bad when dealing with an insecure dog. The trick is to get the dog to want and ask for your attention, not the other way around.

So, the husband's task for that week was this: Ignore Fletch. Fletch no longer exists to anyone in this home. There will be no eye contact, there will be no talking, and you will not approach or acknowledge that Fletch is even in the home. What I did want the man of the house to do is when Fletch is within eye contact of him, just drop something very appealing, like steak, or chicken, Fletch's favorite treats, and just keep walking away. Don't look to see if he takes it. Don't try to get his attention, don't show him what you are dropping. Just continue to do this a few times a day. This will create a positive association without putting any pressure on Fletch.

Within a couple of days Fletch was looking for something to fall from the owner. Getting closer and more curious, the fear had now turned into anticipation. At this point I did not allow the owner to push himself on Fletch, I was still waiting for Fletch to be the pushy one demanding more food from the man just a couple of days ago he would not go near. Within one week of doing this Fletch was going on walks with John, his owner and life was good. This is when I started working with Fletch so we could take him to the next level as a team which we were able to do very easily.

This dog was just purely misunderstood and labeled by people who lack the knowledge or ability to do anything about it. Fear needs to be treated very carefully and a dog cannot overcome such psychological issues through obedience or corrections. It takes a psychological approach to heal the mind.

A few months later I was contacted by the owner and asked if I would come speak to a group of Wolfhound owners and work with their dogs, many of which were rescues with issues. I accepted the offer and that led to my favorite day of training.

I arrived at my client's house to find a bunch of people and 14 giant Irish Wolfhounds in the living room to where I would begin to speak and answer questions about my philosophy of dog training. As you can imagine, it was an impressive sight to see these dogs in one house. We spoke for a while and I answered questions about everything dog related but of course behavioral issues were the main topic.

One owner had a lot of questions about her female that was supposedly very aggressive and would attack for no reason. First, there is no such thing as for no reason, there is always a reason. I asked where the aggressive dog was and she pointed to the only dog sleeping on the floor in the middle of this giant pack. I just laughed thinking they were joking, but they were serious. I explained to all in attendance that the dog being blamed for these fights was by no means aggressive. She may be starting fights but it is not due to her being an aggressive dog, or there is no way she would be crammed into this small space and fall asleep.

Many disputed my claim, especially the owner. At this time, my client suggested that we go outside so I could maybe demonstrate what I do with all the dogs in the yard. We all hung out in the yard watching the dogs interact and just be themselves. Whenever I spotted something I did not like I would point it out and stop the dog that was creating the behavior and continue to speak, and watch, and speak, and watch. You get the picture. Nothing major was happening but what I did notice was most of the owners just oblivious to the little things that matter. The behavior and the way the dogs interacted with each other and the handlers but this is common amongst dog owners and even most trainers. Many of these dogs if not all were rescues and a big mistake people make with rescue dogs is feeling sorry for their past and dwelling on it instead of moving forward and providing the leadership that all dogs need.

As I worked with all the dogs, the owner with the so called aggressive female continued to disagree with me about the aggression issues. I informed her that something she is doing or not doing is causing the bad behavior in her dog. As she is getting more annoyed and arguing her point her two other Wolfhounds are very rudely pushing her from behind for her attention and she is giving it. As they continue to push her hand she continues to pet them as she talks to me and now I am seeing the problem. Once again, the other dogs, not the subject dog is creating leadership issues within the household, but I am not saying anything.

Then in a frustrated tone, the argumentative owner tells me that all she knows is that when she acquired the female, the dog was in such bad shape she had to give her a great deal of care and she controlled everything around the dog. She did not let the other two get away with anything. At that moment, I turned around with my eyebrows raised looking at all the other owners as they all let out a long haaaaa. I looked at the owner and said repeat what you just said. She looked at me and in a more pissed off tone repeated what she said. At that moment, the light bulb went off and she started crying. She finally understood that her lack of boundaries and leadership with her two other dogs was causing the female to handle things on her own. It was a beautiful moment.

Shortly after that we were ending our day. Everyone was thanking me and seemed so appreciative. I really felt blessed. As I was leaving just about to exit the yard, I heard a big fight break out and the owners screaming and panicking. I ran back in and started trying to figure out what was going on and separating or stopping dogs from attacking anything around them. I noticed a dog that was attacked in the far corner of the yard being held and coddled by the owners. It was a young dog and was attacked bad and was shaking in fear as the owners were hugging and telling him that it's ok. I snatched the dog from the owners and went back into the group of dogs, literally kicking or punching anything that came near him. You can't coddle this dog from what happened or there is a good chance it will cause him big problems in the future, fear base aggression or just plain old fear of other dogs. It all happened so fast, but the purpose here was to show the dog that it did not need to fear anything. I had control of him, myself, and every dog around us. Just as important all the other dogs had to see the same thing. There were no grudges here, everything settled down at went back to normal.

What had happened was that when I was leaving, this young dog put his front paws up on the back of another dog. When another older male saw that, and none of the owners addressed that bad behavior, the dogs stepped in and took care of business themselves. It is that simple. If you do not take full leadership and control in that type of situation the dogs will, and it will never be good. If any of the owners would have corrected the young male this would not have happened, but to be honest it was a tremendous learning experience for all that witnessed it.

I am proud to say that recently Suzanne, Fletch's owner sent me pictures of Fletch and informed me that Fletch is now competing and winning in the show ring. The same dog that the family could not be around. It's a beautiful thing and I am forever grateful for Suzanne and John for allowing me to be part of this.

Looking back now on that incredible day I just realized that all that progress was made without ever giving a command. Powerful stuff.

HANDS OFF, NO CONFLICT, AGGRESSION REHABILITATION

What is Hands Off No Conflict Aggression Rehabilitation? It is a form of working with dogs that are extremely aggressive toward people, and I started it by complete accident.

One day I showed up for a first lesson with a male mixed breed that according to the owners was very aggressive toward people and dogs. It has been my experience that people usually think that the problem is much worse than it really is but in this case, it was bad. They lived in a busy apartment complex in Nashville, Tennessee which made the situation even worse because there were people and dogs everywhere. When I arrived, I saw a young couple exit the complex with a dog pulling them on a leash. As soon as the dog spotted me from across the parking lot he went crazy, barking and lunging and trying to get to me. This was my new client.

It was too difficult to talk to the owners so I had them put the dog away so we could go over things. The owners were determined to do e collar training even though I told them I do not rehabilitate aggression with the e collar. To be honest, at this point I was just really burnt out from dealing with **aggression** so I decided to take a different route. Usually I address the aggression separate from the obedience and e collar work, but not this time.

First, as I do with all clients, I teach the use of the e collar by role playing with the owners. I have them hold the e collar in their hand and I teach as if they were the dog so they understand the timing and proper mechanics. Then once they understand it at that level I hold the e collar and I have them work me as if I am the dog. This works great because I can feel if they are doing what they should be doing and if the timing is correct. Also, it allows me to not always cooperate and teach them how to work through it. This allows them to make mistakes on me and not the dog. Once I was comfortable with their e collar use I had them place the collar on the dog but I held the remote.

First I had them do some luring with food and started the dog on a marker word that would be used during the training. Once the dog caught on to that it was time to start conditioning the dog to the e collar and combining the use of the e collar with the marking and rewarding. We did this with me controlling the remote from a safe distance that did not get the dog worked up by my presence. The dog did fantastic and by the end of the session I was close, about 10 yards away without the dog wanting to hurt me and his focus on the owner was great.

The owners continued the training for that week until we met one week later. During the second session, we worked on the recall a little more and added the send away or place command. Again, this was done by me verbally instructing the owners on what to do and again it went very smoothly without the dog ever getting aggressive toward me. During that second week, the owners continued to work on what we went over and started using the e collar for all the basic commands.

It was not until our third and final session that I introduced my dog and worked the client dog using a combination of Behavior Adjustment Training and Constructional Aggression Treatment. By the end of the session I was getting within 5 feet of the dog with my dog next to me and the only reaction from the client's aggressive dog was looking at my client waiting for a reward. The following week this dog came to his first group class and I squatted down after a few minutes of lecture with this dog coming to me for a lick and a hug. What a great feeling. I rehabilitated this dog without ever placing my hands on this dog and avoiding all conflict. The best part about this was that the dog was not only accepting to me but from that day on was accepting to all strangers, even in his home.

I still work with mostly aggressive dogs. The only difference is now when I have a severely people aggressive dog, I use this hands-off approach every time and so far, it has not failed me. It is a lot less stress on both me and the subject dog and I love it. Give it a try.

For training videos visit my YouTube channel:
https://www.youtube.com/user/lklencho

or visit my website at:
http://www.Pakmasters.com

THE E COLLAR IS A CELL PHONE

THE PRONG COLLAR IS A STEERING WHEEL

THE CLICKER IS A BIG FREAKIN PARTY

CALL YOUR DOG AND STEER HIM TO THE BIG FREAKIN PARTY

Thank you to everyone in the dog world that has influenced me over the years. Thank you to every client that has put their trust in me with such a huge responsibility. I have never taken that lightly. I have made and kept beautiful friendships with so many of you.

Thank you to all the dog folks out there that have given me tremendous support over the years. I owe you all so much. I never dreamed I would have a voice in this beautiful industry, but because of you I do. I'll do my best to never let you down.

Most of all I must thank my family. Without you I have nothing. Sophia and Renzo, before I am a Special Agent, before I am a Dog Trainer, I am your dad. The greatest privilege on earth.

Sophia, there are not enough words. You are my sidekick and the best helper anyone could ever ask for. You're always there to not only film but keep me grounded. Your advice and opinion are cherished by me. I know one day you will be famous at whatever you choose to do.

To my wife, Stephanie. It is simple. Everything I have today is because of you. You have sacrificed from day one and pushed me to chase my dreams while never once letting up. You are simply the best human being I have ever known. THANK YOU

I AM A BLESSED MAN

Happy Training Everyone!

Made in the USA
Middletown, DE
04 September 2023

37916857R00038